JOKE BOOK

Scholastic Children's Books
Euston House, 24 Eversholt Street
London, NW1 1DB

A division of Scholastic Ltd
London ~ New York ~ Toronto ~ Sydney ~ Auckland
Mexico City ~ New Delhi ~ Hong Kong

Published in the UK by Scholastic UK Ltd, 2006

Over The Hedge TM & © 2006 DreamWorks Animation L.L.C

10 digit ISBN: 0 439 95121 6
13 digit ISBN: 978 0439 95121 0

Printed by Nørhaven Paperback A/S, Denmark

2 4 6 8 10 9 7 5 3 1

JOKE BOOK

by
Dereen Taylor

■SCHOLASTIC

Verne

The slow and steady leader of
the family, he will need to come
out of his shell to compete
with the charismatic RJ.

RJ

This rowdy raccoon is a charming
con-man who doesn't have a heart
– until he's faced with breaking
the hearts of the forest friends.

Hammy

Bright-eyed and bushy-tailed, Hammy, the crazy rabbit-squirrel, behaves a little nutty most of the time!

Stella

Stella Stinkarella's a femme who's ready to get fatal – until she discovers that maybe everything's not always black and white ...

Ozzie

Ozzie's dying to know if his special talent of 'playing possum' could save the Critter Crew from danger...

Heather

Like most sixteen-year-olds, Heather's dead embarrassed about her father.

Penny and Lou

There's nothing prickly about this pair of rock-solid peas in a pod – even after a sleepless winter looking after three manic porcupups!

WELCOME TO SUBURBIA!

Good News

- The beautifully manicured gardens are full of sweet-smelling flowers to appeal to busy bees and dragonflies everywhere.

- Local teens enjoy keeping fit playing energetic games of roller hockey.

- There's a Homeowners Association looking after all the residents needs.

- Street sweepers patrol the streets at regular intervals to keep them clean and litter-free.

- Suburban humans are friendly to animals.

It really depends
which side of the hedge you're on when it
comes to the pros and cons of life in the suburbs…

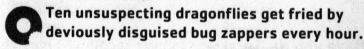

Bad News

 Ten unsuspecting dragonflies get fried by deviously disguised bug zappers every hour.

 A turtle in the wrong place at the wrong time makes a very good hockey puck.

 Gladys Sharp is the president, and she's noticed the lawn at number 10 is 0.4 inches over regulation height.

 Street sweepers don't just suck up litter.

 The animals they are friendly to are Tiger, the hostile Persian cat, and Nugent, the 'playful' rottweiler.

REPTIDIDDILICIOUS JOKES

Why did Verne cross the road?

To get to the Shell garage.

Have you heard of the turtle with no left side?

He's all RIGHT now.

Why is Turtle Wax so expensive?

Because turtles have such tiny ears.

What do you call a turtle in the sky?

A shelli-copter.

TO MAKE YOU CRACK UP

What's Verne's favourite item of clothing?

His turtleneck.

What do turtles have that no other animals have?

Baby turtles.

How long should a turtle's legs be?

Long enough to touch the ground.

For Tiger

The esscential guide to impressing Stella Stinkerella

Call her on her smell-ular phone to let her know how you feel.

Give her flowers. Something's got to smell sweet.

Never ask her what's she's stinking. A foxy skunk deserves her own private thoughts.

Choose carefully if you're taking her to a movie. You don't want her to think it stinks.

Want to stop her smelling?
Hold her nose.

Try not to offend her. She has the power to gas you so hard, your grandchildren will stink.

If you buy her a book, make sure it's a best-smeller.

Tell her she looks scentsational.

Finally, remember, under every stinky girl skunk is a femme ready to get fatal!

JUST A LITTLE MAMMAL HUMOUR
(FROM RJ)

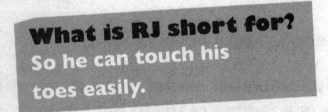

What is RJ short for?
So he can touch his toes easily.

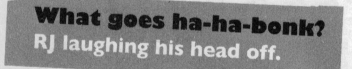

What goes ha-ha-bonk?
RJ laughing his head off.

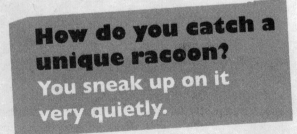

How do you catch a unique racoon?
You sneak up on it very quietly.

Why did RJ push to the front of the queue?
He liked a bit of RJ-bargy.

KNOCK, KNOCK JOKES

Quillo: Knock, Knock

Verne: Who's there?

Quillo: A little porcupup

Verne: A little porcupup who?

Quillo: A little porcupup who can't reach the cookies on the top shelf!

Knock, Knock

Who's there?

Hammy

Hammy who?

Hammy my coat, and I'll be off!

Vincent: Knock, Knock

RJ: Who's there?

Vincent: Irina

RJ: Irina who?

Vincent: You Irina lot of trouble?

I'D RATHER BE

... 'Being mistaken for an amphibian. I'm a reptile actually. It's a common mistake.' Verne

... 'Searching for a Mr Right with a poor sense of smell.' Stella

... 'Helping Mom prick up berries to fill the Log.' Porcupups

HIBERNATING THAN . . .

... 'Squirreling around looking for nuts.' Hammy

... 'Standing next to Stella when she kicks up a stink.' Ozzie

... 'Dying with embarrassment when my Dad plays possum. Again.' Heather

Wild Life

What do you call a squirrel who tosses and turns through the winter?

A hyper-nator.

How do you know Hammy sleeps like a log?

You can hear him sawing.

What is Heather's favourite day of the week to sleep?

Snooze-day.

Do bears snore?

Only when they're asleep.

What happens when Ozzie gets lost in the foggy forest?
He's mist.

Why did the possum cross the road?
It was the chicken's day off.

How does a turtle get up a tree?
It sits on an acorn and waits for it to grow.

How does a turtle get down from a tree?
It sits on a leaf and waits for it to fall.

What's Heather's favourite thing to do in maths class?
Plus-sums.

TOTALLY FUROCIOUS

One day RJ led Hammy over the hedge to ambush the Trail Guide Gals cookie delivery trolley. As soon as Hammy saw the trolley piled high with delicious Love Handles, Skinny Mints and Smackeroons, he was totally over-excited and ready to try out whatever plan RJ had in mind. With a little tuition from RJ, he had transformed himself into the role of a vicious man-eating rabid squirrel. The Trail Guide Gals fled and the piles of cookies were there for the taking. RJ and Hammy were emboldened. Next they targeted an unattended car full of grocery bags. RJ and Hammy's mouths began to water. Just then, Nugent the friendly neighbourhood rottweiler came bounding round the corner.

'Uh-oh, we have an animal problem,'
RJ exclaimed as he whipped out a
pair of training shoes and put them
on in thirty seconds flat.
'Do you think they'll help you outrun
him?' panted Hammy.
'Who knows?' RJ replied. 'I don't have
to outrun him, I only have to outrun
you, my forest friend!'

THE
LOG LIBRARY

Vincent, The Totally Furocious Bear
By R U Scared

How to Be a Crazy Rabbit-Squirrel
By I M Nutts

Playing Possum the Ozman Way
By Di Degaine

Heather's Tale – Dying with Embarrassment
By Rosie Cheeks

Verne's Guide to Suburban Life
By Howard I No

NUTTY JOKES FOR CRAZY RABBIT-SQUIRRELS

WHAT DOES HAMMY DO IF HIS TAIL GROWS TOO LONG?
Ties it in a nut.

WHAT'S THE BEST WAY TO CATCH A SQUIRREL?
Climb up a tree and act nuts.

WHAT DOES HAMMY USE TO BUILD A HOUSE?
Walnuts.

How did Hammy get on TV?
He sat on it.

What do you get if you take the eyes out of squirrels?
Squrrels.

Why did Hammy stand on his head?
Because his feet were tired.

LOVELY DAY FOR A PICNIC

One day, Verne and all the family decide to visit a special spot in the forest that's the perfect place for a picnic. Lou and Penny pack the hamper full of goodies — sandwiches, crisps, cookies and cartons of juice.

The picnic area is 1 mile away. With Verne creeping along and a heavy picnic hamper to carry, it takes the critter crew almost an hour to get there.

When they arrive, everyone's hungry and thirsty, and RJ can't wait to start on the picnic. When Stella unpacks the hamper, she sees they've forgotten to bring the drinks.

The hungry crew of critters are distraught.

'I don't think this is the time to panic...' Verne reassures them.

The forest friends plead with Verne to go back and get the drinks. At first he refuses, because he thinks they'll have eaten everything by the time he returns. But when the family solemnly promise not to touch even a morsel, good old Verne agrees to go.

He sets off, slow and steady.

Two hours later and still there's no sign of Verne. The animals are hungry, but a promise is a promise and nobody eats anything.

After another hour Hammy is looking anything but bright-eyed and bushy-tailed and the porcupups are wailing, 'We're hungry Mama.'

RJ finally yells 'I'm a mover and a shaker and I need food!' He lifts the lid of the hamper, takes out a yummy Skinny Mint cookie and raises it to his mouth to take a big bite.

Just at that second, Verne pops out from behind a nearby rock and says, 'Good job I'm still here to keep an eye on you guys!'

PRICKLY JOKES TO TICKLE

On which side does Lou have the most spikes?
The outside.

Why do porcupines scratch themselves?
They're the only ones who know exactly where it itches.

What do you call a homesick pig?
A porky-pine.

YOUR SENSE OF HUMOUR

What do you call a porcupine with no legs?
A hairbrush.

What do you get if you cross a porcupine with a giraffe?
A six-foot toothbrush.

What do you call two porcupines?
A prickly pair.

WATCHING A FILM AT RJ'S PLACE

The forest friends want RJ to really feel at home. Quillo, Spike and Bucky have hooked up a TV, Hammy's snapped open a soda so RJ can relax, put his feet up and choose a movie...

Verne: Teenage Mutant Ninja Turtles

RJ: The Mask of Zorro

Stella: Austin Flowers

The Porcupups: Empire Spikes Back

Tiger: The Santa Claws

Hammy: The Nutty Professor

Ozzie: Die Hard I, Die Hard II, Die Hard III...
Mission: Impossumble

Lou and Penny: The Spike Who Loved Me

Vincent: Forest Grump

Heather: The Wizard of Ozman

Stella Lets Rip

What did Stella say when the wind blew in the opposite direction?
It's all coming back to me now.

How many skunks does it take to stink out a room?
A phew.

Why did the two skunks argue?
They wanted to kick up a stink.

What's black and white and makes a lot of noise?
A skunk with a drum kit.

What's black, white, black, white, black, white?
A skunk rolling down a hill.

If RJ's serious about winning over his new forest friends, maybe the rowdy raccoon should root around in his golf bag and dig out a few special gifts…

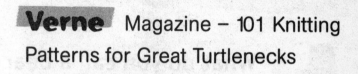 **Verne** Magazine – 101 Knitting Patterns for Great Turtlenecks

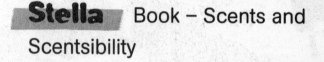 **Stella** Book – Scents and Scentsibility

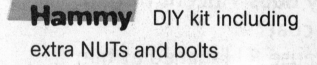 **Hammy** DIY kit including extra NUTs and bolts

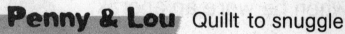 **Penny & Lou** Quillt to snuggle up under

Heather Hair Die

Ozzie Play Station-ary

THE JOKES VINCENT CANNOT BEAR

What do you call a bear without an ear?
B.

Why does Vincent have a fur coat?
Because RJ laughed at him when he wore an anorak.

What kind of bears love to go out in the rain?
Drizzly bears.

Why should you never take Vincent to the zoo?
He prefers the cinema.

What do you get from a bad-tempered bear?
As far away as possible.

Why doesn't Vincent wear socks?
Because he likes to walk in bear feet.

LET'S EAT!

One sniff of a nacho cheese-flavour crisp and the critter crew are ready to ditch the berries! But good old Verne's hanging in there, nibbling away at bark. Maybe this Turtlelicious Menu will tempt him out of his shell!

Starter
Verne's Mexican Shell-fish Platter
A medley of shell-fish served with salsa
and a basket of turt-illa chips.

Hammy's Nutty Bits
Pieces of butter-nut squash drizzled with
nut-cho cheese and coco-nut dressing.

Main Course
RJ's Double Cheese Burglar and Chips
A succulent 1/2 pound burglar served
with extra relish or bear if preferred.

Vincent's Famous Tagliateddy
Ribbons of pasta smothered in a tasty
fur-cheese sauce. The portions are large,
so this one's for those with growling tummies!

Dessert
Lou and Penny's Spine-apple Surprise
The surprise is the sprinkling of prickled
onions on top.

Reptididdilicious!

Stella – Service please!

Waiter – I'm sorry Madam, I really can't take your odour.

Verne – I thought there was a choice of desserts?

RJ – There is.

Verne – There isn't. There's only one.

RJ – Well, you can choose to eat it or leave it.

Knock, Knock

Who's there?

Stella

Stella who?

Stella lot of cookies to eat, so tuck in, my forest friends!

Knock, Knock

Who's there?

Lou

Lou who?

Lou-se the berries and crack open aother bag of those tortilla chips!

FOOD FIGHT!

How do you know hamburgers are male?

Because they're boygers not girlgers.

How do you make a hamburger smile?

Pickle it gently.

Why was the hot dog feeling chuffed?

He was on a roll.

Why didn't the hot dog want to star in the movies?

The rolls weren't good enough.

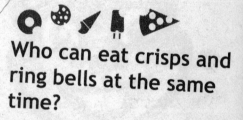

Who can eat crisps and ring bells at the same time?

The Crunch-back of Notre Dame.

Dumpster Diving

HOW DO YOU STOP JUNK FOOD GOING OFF?

Eat it.

WHAT CHEESE IS NOT YOURS?

Nacho cheese.

WHAT'S WORSE THAN FINDING A FLY IN THE LAST MOUTHFUL OF COOKIE?

Finding half a fly in the last mouthful of cookie.

WHY DID THE COOKIE GO TO THE DOCTOR'S?

It felt crummy.

The Critter Crew Quiz

What makes Verne's tail tingle?

A A good slow-and-steady hit on the radio.

B RJ handing out the crisps.

What's a couch potato?

A A spud in the shape of a sofa.

B A human stuffing his face in front of the TV.

What's missing from Hammy's crisp-shaped piece of bark sprinkled with pollen?

A A reason to eat it.

B A nacho cheese glow.

Heather is more likely to...

A Roll a die and get six.

B Die with embarrassment.

What's the exterminator's real name?

A Albie Bach.

B Dwayne La Fontaine.

What's the definition of a sugar rush?

A A packet of Smackeroon cookies in a hurry.

B Hammy, the crazy rabbit-squirrel with a half-eaten cookie and a buzz at the back of his head.

What is Lou and Penny's unique quill skill?

A Picking up soundwaves for Radio Suburbia.

B Skewering hot dogs off the BBQ.

What's Stella most likely to say to Tiger?

A 'Are you the king of the jungle?'

B 'Back off or I'll let rip!'

The Critter Crew Quiz

Answers

Mostly As   Oh dear. Have you been hibernating? You need a sharp jab from The Depletor Turbo to wake you up.

Mostly Bs   Congratulations! You've impressed the critter crew! Welcome to the family. Crack open a family-sized pack of Smackeroon cookies to celebrate.

Mostly Cs   Were you doing the right quiz? Are you sure you weren't doing the Shrek quiz?

ANIMALS

WITH

What did Steve say to Heather and Ozzie?

'Hey, U2, I'm the 'Edge.'

Why did Hammy call the hedge Steve?

Have you ever heard of a hedge called Dave?

Who wears a coat when it's cold and pants when it's hot?

Nugent

What's Vincent's favourite song?

Jingle Bells

ATTITUDE

Why did Stella say 'meow'?

She was learning Purr-sian.

What did Penny say to the potted cactus?

Lou, honey, what are you doing standing in a pot?

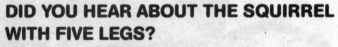

Bright-eyed and Bushy-tailed

DID YOU HEAR ABOUT THE SQUIRREL WITH FIVE LEGS?
His trousers fit him like a glove.

WHAT FOLLOWS HAMMY EVERYWHERE HE GOES?
His tail.

IF YOU FIND RABBITS IN RABBIT HOLES, WHERE DO YOU FIND SQUIRRELS?
In square'oles.

WHAT DO SQUIRRELS EAT IN SPACE?
Astro-nuts.

WHAT HAPPENED TO THE SQUIRREL WHO SWALLOWED A FIREFLY?
He went nutty with de-light.

Stella Stinkarella

What's black and white and red all over?
An embarrassed skunk.

What did Verne say to Stella?
Say it, don't spray it.

How much does it cost to buy an American skunk?
One scent.

What smells bad and sniffs in the corner?
A skunk with a cold.

What do you call a religious skunk?
A munk.

WHAT HAPPENED WHEN...

WHAT HAPPENED WHEN HAMMY DRANK EIGHT CANS OF COLA?

He brought seven up.

WHAT HAPPENED WHEN TIGER SWITCHED ON THE DVD PLAYER?

He pressed paws.

WHAT HAPPENED WHEN VERNE SAW A GHOST IN THE FOREST?

He was turtley shell-shocked.

WHAT HAPPENED WHEN OZZIE'S PANTS FELL DOWN?

He died of embarrassment.

WHAT HAPPENED WHEN RJ CREPT INTO VINCENT'S CAVE?

He ran out with a bear behind.

WHAT HAPPENED WHEN STELLA WENT ON HOLIDAY?

She packed everything including the kitchen stink.

What would

If I were an item of
clothing, I'd be a shell suit.
Verne

If I were a
perfume, I'd be
scentsational.
Stella

If I were a book,
I'd be a furry tail.
Hammy

If I were something to eat,
I'd be a quick bite.
Nugent

you be?

If I were a country, I'd be Australia.
Ozzie

If I were a colour,
I'd be purple.
Heather

If I were in a band,
I'd play purr-cussion.
Tiger

Don't miss these totally furocious colouring and activity books

0 439 95117 8 **£3.99**

0 439 95118 6 **£3.99**